The Oxford Book of Descants

Melody edition

Edited by Julian Elloway

MUSIC DEPARTMENT

OXFORD
UNIVERSITY PRESS

OXFORD

UNIVERSITY PRESS

Great Clarendon Street, Oxford OX2 6DP,
United Kingdom

Oxford University Press is a department of the University of Oxford.
It furthers the University's objective of excellence in research, scholarship,
and education by publishing worldwide. Oxford is a registered trade mark of
Oxford University Press in the UK and in certain other countries

First published 2012

ISBN 978-0-19-338680-8

Music origination by Julian Elloway
Printed in Great Britain on acid-free paper by
Caligraving Ltd, Thetford, Norfolk.

PREFACE

Although the hymn descant may be traced from the Renaissance practice of fauxbourdon, where the cantus firmus, or plainchant melody, appeared in the tenor below one or more upper parts, the modern practice of putting an extra line above a tune already in the top part appears to date from the early twentieth century. Notable early publications include Athelstan Riley's 1916 *A Collection of Faux-Bourdons and Descants for the French Ecclesiastical Melodies and other Tunes in the English Hymnal* (the earliest printed collection with 'Descant' in its title, as far as I am aware) and Alan Gray's 1920 *A Book of Descants* (Gray was for 37 years organist of Trinity College, Cambridge, the first of a distinguished list of Cambridge descant composers). Among hymn books, *Songs of Praise* (1925 and 1931) included a number of descant and fauxbourdon settings and, in 1950, *Hymns Ancient & Modern Revised* included descants (many by Sydney H Nicholson), alongside the fauxbourdon settings of earlier editions. At King's College, Cambridge, the carol arrangements of David Willcocks and his successors, recorded and broadcast in carol services, have broadened the popularity of the descant. Sir David's distinguished contribution, starting with the descants included in the original 1961 *Carols for Choirs*, continues to the present day, and I am delighted to have been able to include some of the more recent of these.

This collection includes a range of descants from those of Gray and Nicholson, Edward Bairstow, William Harris, and Harold Darke, right through to the twenty-first century with many newly commissioned items. In between there is a selection from a wide variety of sources, some long established and others recently published. Overall, the preference is for descants that draw attention to the words and not to themselves, that are sensitive to the words with which they are most frequently sung, and that are written with sympathy to the idiom of the original hymn melody (sometimes by the composer of the original hymn). That said, there are also a few striking examples whose effect is partly caused by their notably different harmonic idiom.

Some descants work well for choral festivals and services where the choir is the focus of attention, and others are particularly appropriate for broadcast services where the effect is heard by a non-singing audience. However, the descants selected for this collection are intended for ordinary use in worship where, although sung by and enjoyed by the choir, they are to be appreciated by the congregation, enhancing the meaning of the words and intensifying the sung prayer of the worshipper. This is a heavy responsibility for those choosing descants. It also means that they should be rehearsed, be sung well, and be considered no less important than every other part of the service. Less is more: there is no need automatically to sing a descant to a hymn just because the descant is known. The fewer descants in a service, the more special and important is each; it is better to allow every one to be significant and telling.

Although the texts that are shown here with the music are mostly final verses, descants need not always be sung to the last verse. Nor need they invariably be sung fortissimo throughout. They are part of a wider repertoire for providing variety and illuminating the words that includes unison verses (tutti, or upper voices or lower voices—with or without alternative harmonies), verses that are unaccompanied after the opening bars, or verses that are accompanied by different combinations of instruments or organ without pedals. Some descants are effective if tenors also sing the descant an octave lower. Many of the best descants are written specifically for, and indeed only 'work' for, one set of words and not for others to which the same tune may be sung. In two cases we have given the same tune twice, with different words and different descants for each.

Descants generally work best with a melody that has a strong bass line, preferably played on an organ with an independent pedal section. This means that folk tunes, Taizé chants, etc. are often unsuitable for a descant. Similarly, many recent worship songs require a more flexible approach from the choir and instrumentalists that is outside the scope of this anthology; however, this collection does include a number of folk melodies and worship songs that lend themselves to a conventional descant treatment.

The descants in this volume are mostly unison, but with occasional extra parts, especially in final bars. A second key is presented where both keys are widely used and the descant range is still accessible in the higher key. Some descants work with SATB harmonies that may have been used in previous verses, and others with altered harmonies in the specially written organ part, as indicated in the music.

The decision to include a small number of descants that many choir singers know and may already own is justified by the convenience of having these descants within a single volume. Of course, singers will not find all their personal favourites here, but the hope must be that many of the descants included in this volume will soon be added to the list of favourites.

I am grateful to many friends and colleagues who have shared their expertise and experience, in particular from Oxford University Press, the Royal School of Church Music, and the Diocese of Gloucester, to others who have offered valuable suggestions and advice, and to choirs and congregations that have tested the descants in worship.

JULIAN ELLOWAY
Stroud, 2012

CONTENTS

INDEX OF FIRST LINES

The Oxford
Book of Descants

1a ABBOT'S LEIGH (in C)

Glorious things of thee are spoken
Father, Lord of all creation
God is Love: let heaven adore him
Sing we of the blessed Mother

Descant by Antony Baldwin

Sa - viour, if____ of Zi - on's ci - ty I through grace a
Ho - ly Spi - rit, rush - ing, burn - ing wind and flame of
God__ is Love:__ and though with blind - ness sin af - flicts the
Sing__ the chief - est joy of Ma - ry when on earth her

mem - ber am,__ let__ the world__ de - ride or pi - ty,
Pen - te - cost,__ fire__ our hearts__ a - fresh with yearn-ing
souls__ of men,__ God's__ e - ter - nal lov - ing - kind-ness
work__ was done,__ and__ the Lord__ of all cre - a - tion

I will glo - ry in__ thy name;__ fa - ding is the
to re - gain__ what we__ have lost.__ May__ your love u -
holds and guides__ them e - ven then.__ Sin__ and death and
brought her to__ his heaven - ly home:__ vir - gin mo - ther,

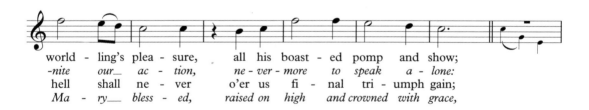

world - ling's plea - sure, all his boast - ed pomp and show;
-nite our__ ac - tion, ne - ver - more to speak a - lone:
hell shall ne - ver o'er us fi - nal tri - umph gain;
Ma - ry__ bless - ed, raised on high and crowned with grace,

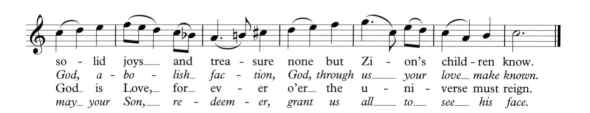

so - lid joys__ and trea - sure none but Zi - on's child - ren know.
God, a - bo - lish_ fac - tion, God, through us__ your love_ make known.
God_ is Love,_ for_ ev - er o'er the u - ni - verse must reign.
may_ your Son,_ re - deem - er, grant us all__ to__ see__ his face.

Abbot's Leigh by Cyril Vincent Taylor (1907–91) © 1942 Oxford University Press
Descant by Antony Baldwin (b. 1957) © 2006 Oxford University Press
First text: 'Glorious things of thee are spoken' by John Newton (1725–1807)
Second text: 'Father, Lord of all creation' by Stewart Cross (1928–89) © Mrs Mary Cross
Third text: 'God is Love: let heaven adore him' by Timothy Rees (1874–1939)
Fourth text: 'Sing we of the blessed Mother' by George B Timms (1910–97) © Oxford University Press

1b ABBOT'S LEIGH (in D)

Glorious things of thee are spoken
Father, Lord of all creation
God is Love: let heaven adore him
Sing we of the blessed Mother

Descant by Antony Baldwin

Sa - viour, if of Zi - on's ci - ty I through grace a
Ho - ly Spi - rit, rush - ing, burn - ing wind and flame of
God is Love: and though with blind - ness sin af - flicts the
Sing the chief - est joy of Ma - ry when on earth her

mem - ber am, let the world de - ride or pi - ty,
Pen - te - cost, fire our hearts a - fresh with yearn - ing
souls of men, God's e - ter - nal lov - ing - kind - ness
work was done, and the Lord of all cre - a - tion

I will glo - ry in thy name; fa - ding is the
to re - gain what we have lost. May your love u -
holds and guides them e - ven then. Sin and death and
brought her to his heaven - ly home: vir - gin mo - ther,

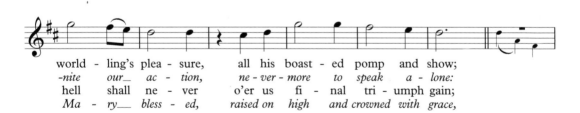

world - ling's plea - sure, all his boast - ed pomp and show;
-nite our ac - tion, ne - ver - more to speak a - lone:
hell shall ne - ver o'er us fi - nal tri - umph gain;
Ma - ry bless - ed, raised on high and crowned with grace,

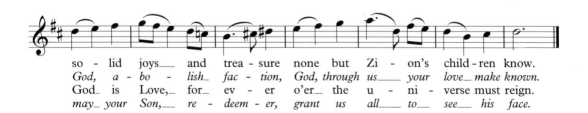

so - lid joys and trea - sure none but Zi - on's child - ren know.
God, a - bo - lish fac - tion, God, through us your love make known.
God is Love, for ev - er o'er the u - ni - verse must reign.
may your Son, re - deem - er, grant us all to see his face.

Abbot's Leigh by Cyril Vincent Taylor (1907–91) © 1942 Oxford University Press
Descant by Antony Baldwin (b 1957) © 2006 Oxford University Press
First text: 'Glorious things of thee are spoken' by John Newton (1725–1807)
Second text: 'Father, Lord of all creation' by Stewart Cross (1928–89) © Mrs Mary Cross
Third text: 'God is Love: let heaven adore him' by Timothy Rees (1874–1939)
Fourth text: 'Sing we of the blessed Mother' by George B Timms (1910–97) © Oxford University Press

2 ABERYSTWYTH

Jesu, lover of my soul

Descant by Alan Gray

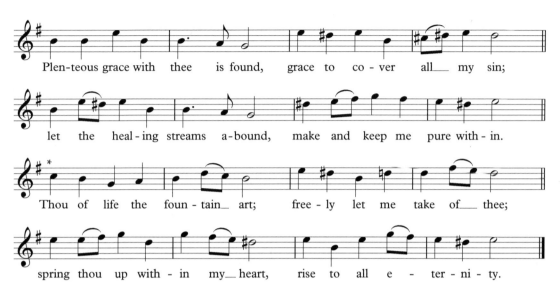

Plen-teous grace with thee is found, grace to co-ver all my sin;

let the heal-ing streams a-bound, make and keep me pure with-in.

Thou of life the foun-tain art; free-ly let me take of thee;

spring thou up with-in my heart, rise to all e-ter-ni-ty.

* As an alternative (and at Alan Gray's suggestion), start the descant at this point.
Aberystwyth by Joseph Parry (1841–1903)
Descant by Alan Gray (1855–1935)
Text: 'Jesu, lover of my soul' by Charles Wesley (1707–88)

3a & b ABRIDGE (in D and C)

Be thou my guardian and my guide

Descant by Christopher Gower

3a in D

Still let me ev-er watch and pray, and feel that I am frail;

that if the tempt-er cross my way, yet he may not pre-vail.

3b in C

Still let me ev-er watch and pray, and feel that I am frail;

that if the tempt-er cross my way, yet he may not pre-vail.

Abridge by Isaac Smith (1734–1805)
Descant by Christopher Gower (b. 1939) © 1990 Kevin Mayhew Ltd. Reproduced by permission; Licence Nr 217011/1
<www.kevinmayhew.com>
Text: 'Be thou my guardian and my guide' by Isaac Williams (1802–65)

4 ADESTE, FIDELES

O come, all ye faithful

Descant by David Willcocks

Sing__ choirs of__ an - gels,____ sing in ex-ul-ta-tion, sing__ all ye

ci - ti - zens of heav'n a - bove, Glo - - - -

- ry in__ the__ high - est: O come,____

O come,____ let us a - dore____ him, Christ the Lord!

Adeste fideles possibly by John Francis Wade (c.1711–86)
Descant by David Willcocks (b. 1919) © 1961 Oxford University Press
Text: 'O come, all ye faithful' translated by Frederick Oakeley (1802–80) from 18th-century Latin

5 ALLELUIA No. 1

Alleluia, alleluia, give thanks to the risen Lord

Descant by Anthony F Carver
and Donald Davison

Al - le - lu - ia, al - le - lu - ia, give__ thanks to the ri - sen Lord;

al - le - lu - ia, al - le - lu - ia, give__ praise to his name.

Melody and words by Donald E Fishel (b. 1950)
Descant by Anthony F Carver (b. 1947) and Donald Davison (b. 1937)
© 1973 International Liturgy Publications (ILP) PO Box 50476, Nashville, Tennessee 37205 USA. Administered by
Song Solutions CopyCare <www.songsolutions.org>

6a & b ANGEL VOICES (in D and C)
Angel-voices ever singing

Descant by John Cooke

6a in D

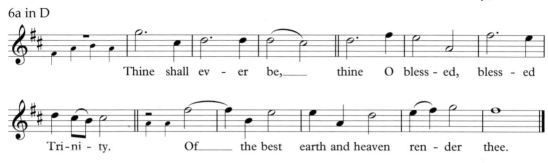

Thine shall ev - er be,___ thine O bless - ed, bless - ed
Tri - ni - ty. Of___ the best earth and heaven ren - der thee.

6b in C

Thine shall ev - er be,___ thine O bless - ed, bless - ed
Tri - ni - ty. Of___ the best earth and heaven ren - der thee.

Angel Voices by E G Monk (1819–1900)
Descant by John Cooke (1930–95) © The Estate of John Cooke
Text: 'Angel-voices ever singing' by Francis Pott (1832–1909)

7a ANIMA CHRISTI (in F)
Soul of my Saviour, sanctify my breast

Descant by David Willcocks

Guard and de - fend me from the foe ma - lign, in___ death's dread mo - ments
make me on - ly___ thine; call___ me and___ bid me come to thee on
high where I may praise thee with thy saints for___ ay.

Anima Christi by William Maher (1823–77)
Descant by David Willcocks (b. 1919) © 2012 Oxford University Press
Text: 'Soul of my Saviour, sanctify my breast' — anonymous translation of 14th-century Latin

7b ANIMA CHRISTI (in G)

Soul of my Saviour, sanctify my breast

Descant by David Willcocks

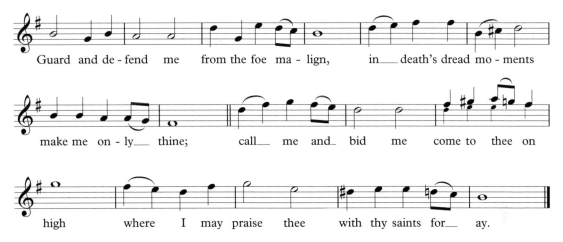

Guard and de-fend me from the foe ma-lign, in death's dread mo-ments make me on-ly thine; call me and bid me come to thee on high where I may praise thee with thy saints for ay.

Anima Christi by William Maher (1823–77)
Descant by David Willcocks (b. 1919) © 2012 Oxford University Press
Text: 'Soul of my Saviour, sanctify my breast'—anonymous translation of 14th-century Latin

8 AURELIA

The Church's one foundation

Descant by Adrian Lucas

Yet she on earth hath u-nion with God the Three in One, and sweet com-mu-nion with those whose rest is won: O hap-py, ho-ly! Lord, give us grace, like them, the meek and low-ly, on high may dwell with thee.

Aurelia by S S Wesley (1810–76)
Descant by Adrian Lucas (b. 1962) © 2012 Oxford University Press
Text: 'The Church's one foundation' by Samuel J Stone (1839–1900)

9 AUS DER TIEFE (HEINLEIN)

Forty days and forty nights

Descant by James Vivian

Keep, O keep us, Sa-viour dear,— ev-er con-stant by thy— side,

that with thee— we— may— ap-pear at the e-ter-nal Eas-ter-tide.

Aus der Tiefe or *Heinlein* possibly by Martin Herbst (1654–81)
Descant by James Vivian (b. 1974) © 2012 Oxford University Press
Text: 'Forty days and forty nights' by George H Smyttan (1822–70) and Francis Pott (1832–1909)

10a & b AUSTRIA (in E♭ and F)

Praise the Lord! ye heavens, adore him
Glorious things of thee are spoken

Descant by Thomas H Ingham

10a in E♭

Wor-ship, ho-nour, glo-ry, bless-ing, Lord, we— of-fer to thy name;
Sa-viour, if of Zi-on's ci-ty I— through grace a mem-ber am;

young and— old, thy praise ex-press-ing, join their Sa-viour to pro-claim.
let the—world de-ride or pi-ty, I— will glo-ry in thy name.

As the saints in heaven a-dore thee, we would bow be-fore thy— throne;
Fa-ding is the world-ling's plea-sure, all his— boast-ed— pomp and— show;

as thine an-gels serve be-fore thee, so— on— earth thy will be done.
so-lid joys and last-ing trea-sure none but— Zi-on's child-ren know.

10b in F

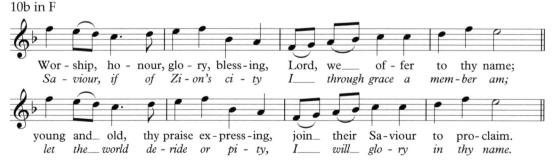

Wor-ship, ho-nour, glo-ry, bless-ing, Lord, we— of-fer to thy name;
Sa-viour, if of Zi-on's ci-ty I— through grace a mem-ber am;

young and— old, thy praise ex-press-ing, join— their Sa-viour to pro-claim.
let the—world de-ride or pi-ty, I— will glo-ry in thy name.

Austria by Franz Joseph Haydn (1732–1809)
Descant by Thomas H Ingham (1878–1948) © 1925 Oxford University Press
First text: 'Praise the Lord! ye heavens, adore him'—third verse by Edward Osler (1798–1863)
Second text: 'Glorious things of thee are spoken' by John Newton (1725–1807)

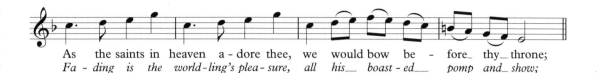

As the saints in heaven a-dore thee, we would bow be - fore_ thy_ throne;
Fa - ding is the world-ling's plea-sure, all his_ boast - ed_ pomp and_ show;

as thine an - gels serve be - fore thee, so_ on_ earth thy will be done.
so - lid joys and last - ing trea-sure none but_ Zi - on's child-ren know.

11 BEAUTY FOR BROKENNESS (GOD OF THE POOR)

Beauty for brokenness

Descant by Ashley Grote

Thoughtfully

Light-en our dark-ness, breathe on this flame,_ un-til your jus-tice burns

bright - ly,_ un - til all_ the na - tions learn of your ways,

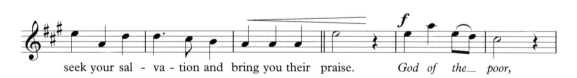

seek your sal - va - tion and bring you their praise. *God of the_ poor,*

friend of the_ weak, give us com - pas-sion we pray: melt our cold hearts, let

tears fall like rain; come, change our love to u flame._

Melody and words by Graham Kendrick (b. 1950)
Descant by Ashley Grote (b. 198?)
© 1993 Graham Kendrick / Make Way Music Ltd, PO Box 320, Tunbridge Wells, TN2 9DE, UK. <www.grahamkendrick.co.uk>
Used by permission

12a & b BLAENWERN (in G and F)

Love divine, all loves excelling
God is here! As we his people

Descant by John Scott

12a in G

(Melody)

Fin - ish then thy new_ cre - a - tion: pure and spot - less let_ us be;
Lord of all, of church and king - dom, in an age of change and doubt,

let us see thy great sal - va - tion per - fect - ly_ re-stored in thee;
keep us faith - ful to_ the gos - pel, help us work_ your pur - pose out.

Descant

changed from glo - ry in - to glo - ry, till_ in heaven we take_ our place,_
Here,_ in this day's de - di - ca - tion, all_ we have to give, re - ceive:

till_ we cast_ our crowns be - fore thee, lost_ in_ won - der, love,_ and praise!
we,_ who can - not live with - out you, we a - dore_ you! We_ be - lieve.

12b in F

(Melody)

Fin - ish then thy new_ cre - a - tion: pure and spot - less let_ us be;
Lord of all, of church and king - dom, in an age of change and doubt,

let us see thy great sal - va - tion per - fect - ly_ re-stored in thee;
keep us faith - ful to_ the gos - pel, help us work_ your pur - pose out.

Descant

changed from glo - ry in - to glo - ry, till_ in heaven we take_ our place,_
Here,_ in this day's de - di - ca - tion, all_ we have to give, re - ceive:

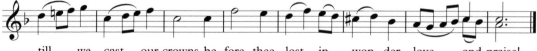

till_ we cast_ our crowns be - fore thee, lost_ in_ won - der, love,_ and praise!
we,_ who can - not live with - out you, we a - dore_ you! We_ be - lieve.

Blaenwern by William P Rowlands (1860–1937)
Descant by John Scott (b. 1956) © 2001 Banks Music Publications. Reproduced by permission
First text: 'Love divine, all loves excelling' by Charles Wesley (1707–88)
Second text: 'God is here! As we his people' by F Pratt Green (1903–2000)

13a & b CARLISLE (in E♭ and D)

Stand up, and bless the Lord

'Tis good, Lord, to be here

Descant by Sydney H Nicholson

13a in E♭

Stand up, and bless the Lord; the Lord your God a - dore;
'Tis good, Lord, to be here! Yet we may not re - main;

stand up, and bless his glo - rious name, hence-forth for ev - er - more.
but since thou bidst us leave the mount, come with us to the plain.

13b in D

Stand up, and bless the Lord; the Lord your God a - dore;
'Tis good, Lord, to be here! Yet we may not re - main;

stand up, and bless his glo - rious name, hence-forth for ev - er - more.
but since thou bidst us leave the mount, come with us to the plain.

Carlisle by Charles Lockhart (1745–1815)
Descant by Sydney H Nicholson (1875–1947) © The Royal School of Church Music. Used by permission
First text: 'Stand up, and bless the Lord' by James Montgomery (1771–1854)
Second text: ''Tis good, Lord, to be here' by J Armitage Robinson (1858–1933)

14 COE FEN

How shall I sing that majesty

Descant by Kenneth Naylor

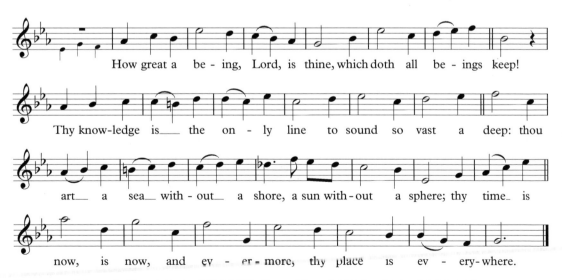

How great a be - ing, Lord, is thine, which doth all be - ings keep!

Thy know-ledge is the on - ly line to sound so vast a deep: thou

art a sea with - out a shore, a sun with - out a sphere; thy time is

now, is now, and ev - er - more, thy place is ev - ery-where.

Hymn tune and descant by Kenneth Naylor (1931–91) © The Estate of Kenneth Nicholson Naylor. Administered by
Oxford University Press
Text: 'How shall I sing that majesty' by John Mason (c.1645–94)

15 CORVEDALE
There's a wideness in God's mercy

Descant by Maurice Bevan

If our love were but more sim - ple, we should take him at his word;___

and our lives would be all glad - ness in the joy of Christ our Lord.
(pres-ence of the Lord.)

Hymn tune and descant by Maurice Bevan (1921–2006)
© 1993 Cathedral Music Ltd, King Charles Cottage, Racton, Chichester, West Sussex PO18 9DT
Text: 'There's a wideness in God's mercy' by Frederick W Faber (1814–63)

16 CRIMOND
The Lord's my shepherd, I'll not want

Descant by Donald Davison

Good - ness___ and mer - cy all___ my life shall sure - ly fol - low me;

and in___ God's house for ev - er - more my dwell-ing - place___ shall be.

Crimond probably by David Grant (1833–93)
Descant by Donald Davison (b. 1937) © 2000 Oxford University Place
Text: 'The Lord's my shepherd, I'll not want' from the *Scottish Psalter* 1650

17a CROSS OF JESUS (in G)
Come, thou long-expected Jesus

Descant by Paul Leddington Wright

By thine own e - ter - nal___ Spi - rit, rule in___ all our hearts a - lone:

ossia

by thine all - suf - fi - cient me - rit___ raise us to thy glo - rious throne.

Cross of Jesus by John Stainer (1840–1901)
Descant by Paul Leddington Wright (b. 1951) © 2012 Oxford University Press
Text: 'Come, thou long-expected Jesus' by Charles Wesley (1707–88)

17b CROSS OF JESUS (in F)

Come, thou long-expected Jesus

Descant by Paul Leddington Wright

By thine own e - ter - nal__ Spi - rit, rule in__ all our hearts a - lone:

by thine all - suf - fi - cient me - rit__ raise us to thy glo - rious throne.

Cross of Jesus by John Stainer (1840–1901)
Descant by Paul Leddington Wright (b. 1951) © 2012 Oxford University Press
Text: 'Come, thou long-expected Jesus' by Charles Wesley (1707–88)

18a & b CRUCIFER (in D and C)

Lift high the cross, the love of Christ proclaim

Descant by Harold Darke

18a in D

Lift high the cross, the love of Christ pro - claim

till all the world a - dore his sa - cred name.

18b in C

Lift high the cross, the love of Christ pro - claim

till all the world a - dore his sa - cred name.

Crucifer by Sydney H Nicholson (1875–1947) © Hymns Ancient & Modern Ltd. Used by permission
Descant by Harold Darke (1888–1976) © The Estate of Harold Darke. Used by permission
Text: 'Lift high the cross' by G W Kitchin (1827–1912) and M R Newbolt (1874–1956)

19 CWM RHONDDA

Guide me, O thou great Redeemer (Jehovah)

Descant by John Scott

When I tread the verge of__ Jor - dan, bid my__ an - xious fears sub-side;_____

death of__ death, and hell's de-struc-tion, land me safe on Ca - naan's side:

songs of prai - ses, songs of prai - ses I_____ will ev - er
(and)   (and)

give_____ to thee, I_____ will ev - er give__ to thee.

Cwm Rhondda by John Hughes (1873–1932)
Descant by John Scott (b. 1956) © 2012 Oxford University Press
Text: 'Guide me, O thou great Redeemer' translated from the Welsh of William Williams (1717–91)

20a DARWALL'S 148th (in D)

Ye holy angels bright

Descant from *Hymns Ancient & Modern Revised*
by Sydney H Nicholson

My soul, bear thou thy__ part, tri - umph in God a - bove,_____

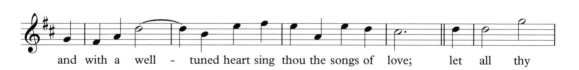

and with a well - tuned heart sing thou the songs of love; let all thy

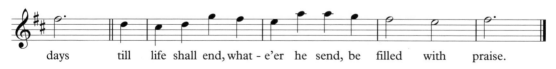

days till life shall end, what - e'er he send, be filled with praise.

Darwall's 148th by John Darwall (1731–89)
Descant from *Hymns Ancient & Modern Revised* by Sydney H Nicholson (1875–1947) © Hymns Ancient & Modern Ltd. Used by permission
Text: 'Ye holy angels bright' by Richard Baxter (1615–91)

20b DARWALL'S 148th (in C)

Ye holy angels bright

Descant from *Hymns Ancient & Modern Revised*
by Sydney H Nicholson

My soul, bear thou thy part, tri - umph in God a - bove,

and with a well - tuned heart sing thou the songs of love; let all thy

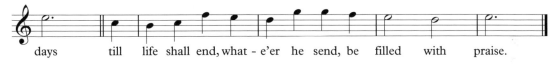

days till life shall end, what - e'er he send, be filled with praise.

Darwall's 148th by John Darwall (1731–89)
Descant from *Hymns Ancient & Modern Revised* by Sydney H Nicholson (1875–1947) © Hymns Ancient & Modern Ltd. Used by permission
Text: 'Ye holy angels bright' by Richard Baxter (1615–91)

21a & b DEUS TUORUM MILITUM (in C and B♭)

Awake, awake: fling off the night

Descant by Simon Lole

21a in C

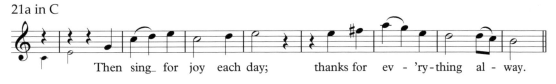

Then sing_ for joy each day; thanks for ev - 'ry-thing al - way.

Lift your hearts; with one ac - cord praise God through Je - sus Christ our Lord.

21b in B♭

Then sing_ for joy each day; thanks for ev - 'ry-thing al - way.

Lift your hearts; with one ac - cord praise God through Je - sus Christ our Lord.

Deus tuorum militum from *Grenoble Antiphoner* 1753
Descant by Simon Lole (b. 1957) © 2012 Oxford University Press
Text: 'Awake, awake: fling off the night' by J R Peacey (1896–1971) © The Revd Mary J Hancock

22a & b DIX (in A♭ and G)

As with gladness men of old

Descant by John Wilson

22a in A♭

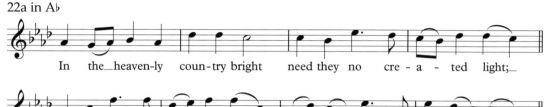

In the heaven-ly coun-try bright need they no cre - a - ted light;

thou its light, its joy, its crown, thou its sun which goes not down;

there for ev - er may we sing al - le - lu - ias to our King.

22b in G

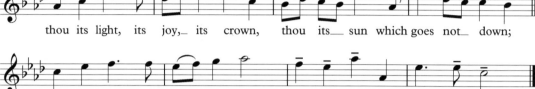

In the heaven-ly coun-try bright need they no cre - a - ted light;

thou its light, its joy, its crown, thou its sun which goes not down;

there for ev - er may we sing al - le - lu - ias to our King.

Dix adapted from a chorale by Conrad Kocher (1786–1872)
Descant by John Wilson (1905–92) © The Estate of John Wilson. Administered by Oxford University Press
Text: 'As with gladness men of old' by William Chatterton Dix (1837–98)

23a DOMINUS REGIT ME (in G)

The King of love my shepherd is

Descant from *Hymns Ancient & Modern*
probably by Sydney H Nicholson

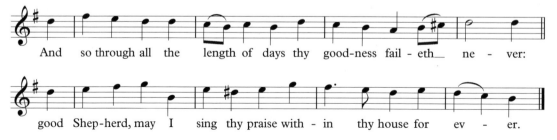

And so through all the length of days thy good-ness fail - eth ne - ver:

good Shep-herd, may I sing thy praise with - in thy house for ev - er.

Dominus regit me by John Bacchus Dykes (1823–76). Descant from *Hymns Ancient & Modern Revised* probably by
Sydney H Nicholson (1875–1947). © Hymns Ancient & Modern Ltd. Used by permission
Text: 'The King of love my shepherd is' by Henry Williams Baker (1821–77)

23b DOMINUS REGIT ME (in F)
The King of love my shepherd is

Descant from *Hymns Ancient & Modern*
probably by Sydney H Nicholson

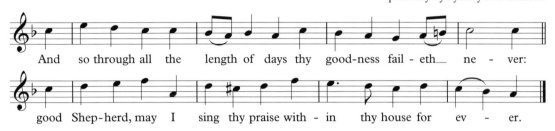

And so through all the length of days thy good-ness fail - eth ne - ver: good Shep-herd, may I sing thy praise with - in thy house for ev - er.

Dominus regit me by John Bacchus Dykes (1823–76). Descant from *Hymns Ancient & Modern Revised* probably by
Sydney H Nicholson (1875–1947). © Hymns Ancient & Modern Ltd. Used by permission
Text: 'The King of love my shepherd is' by Henry Williams Baker (1821–77)

24 DOWN AMPNEY
Come down, O Love divine

Descant by David Willcocks

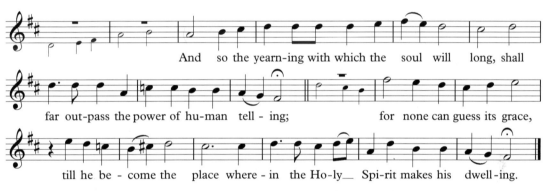

And so the yearn-ing with which the soul will long, shall far out-pass the power of hu-man tell - ing; for none can guess its grace, till he be - come the place where - in the Ho-ly Spi-rit makes his dwell-ing.

Down Ampney by Ralph Vaughan Williams (1872–1958) from *The English Hymnal*. Reproduced by permission of
Oxford University Press. All rights reserved. Descant by David Willcocks (b. 1919) © 2012 Oxford University Press
Text: 'Come down, O Love divine' translated from the Italian of Bianco da Siena (d. 1434)

25 DUKE STREET
Fight the good fight with all thy might
Forth in the peace of Christ we go

Descant by Philip Moore

Faint not nor fear, his arms are near; he chang-eth not, and thou art dear;
We are his Church, he makes us one: here is one hearth for all to find,
We are the Church; Christ bids us show that in his church all na-tions find
on - ly be - lieve, and thou shalt see that Christ is all in all to thee.
here is one flock, one Shep-herd-King, here is one faith, one heart, one mind,
their hearth and home, where Christ re - stores true peace, true love, to all man-kind.
(to hu - man-kind.)

Duke Street attributed to John Hatton (d. 1793). Descant by Philip Moore (b. 1943)
© 1996 Kevin Mayhew Ltd. Reproduced by permission; Licence Nr 217011/1 <www.kevinmayhew.com>
First text: 'Fight the good fight with all thy might' by John S B Monsell (1811–75). Second and third texts: 'Forth in the peace
of Christ we go' by James Quinn (1919–2010) © 1969 & 1987 Continuum International Publishing Group

26 EASTER HYMN

Jesus Christ is risen today, Alleluia

Descant by John Rutter

But the pains that he en - dured, *Al - le-lu - ia, al - le - lu - ia!*

our sal - va - tion have pro - cured; *Al - le-lu - ia, al - le - lu - ia!*

now a - bove the sky he's King, *Al - le - lu - ia!*

where the an - gels ev - er sing.__ *Al - le-lu - ia, al - le - lu - ia!*

Easter Hymn adapted from *Lyra Davidica* 1708
Descant by John Rutter (b. 1945) © 2000 Collegium Music Publications
Text: 'Jesus Christ is risen today, Alleluia' from *Lyra Davidica* 1708

27 EISENACH

O Love, how deep, how broad, how high

The heavenly Word proceeding forth (O saving Victim, opening wide)

Descant by Harrison Oxley

To him whose bound-less love has won sal - va - tion for us through his_Son,
All praise and thanks to thee as-cend for ev - er - more, blessed One_ in_Three;

to God the Fa - ther, glo - ry be both now and_through e - ter - ni - ty.
O grant us life_that shall not end in our_true_ na - tive land with thee.

Eisenach by Johann Schein (1586–1630)
Descant by Harrison Oxley (1933–2009) © 1996 Kevin Mayhew Ltd. Reproduced by permission; Licence Nr 217011/1
<www.kevinmayhew.com>
First text: 'O Love, how deep, how broad, how high' tr. by Benjamin Webb (1819–85) from 15th-century Latin
Second text: 'The heavenly Word, proceeding forth' tr. by John Mason Neale (1818–66) from Thomas Aquinas

28a & b ENGLEBERG (in F and G)

When, in our music, God is glorified

All praise to thee, for thou, O King divine

Descant by David Willcocks

28a in F

Let ev - ery in - stru-ment be tuned for praise!_____ Let all re -
Let_ ev - ery tongue con - fess with one ac - cord_____ in_ heaven and

-joice who have a voice to_ raise!_____ And may_ God give us
earth that Je - sus Christ is_ Lord;_____ and God_ the Fa - ther

cresc.

faith_ to sing al - ways: Al - le - lu - ia!
be_ by all a - dored: Al - le - lu - ia!

28b in G

Let_ ev - ery in - stru-ment be tuned for praise!_____ Let all re -
Let_ ev - ery tongue con - fess with one ac - cord_____ in_ heaven and

-joice who have a voice to_ raise!_____ And may_ God give us
earth that Je - sus Christ is_ Lord;_____ and God_ the Fa - ther

cresc.

faith_ to sing al - ways: Al - le - lu - ia!_____
be_ by all a - dored: Al - le - lu - ia!_____

Engleberg by Charles Villiers Stanford (1852–1924)
Descant by David Willcocks (b. 1919) © 2012 Oxford University Press
First text: 'When, in our music, God is glorified' by F Pratt Green (1903–2000)
Second text: 'All praise to thee, for thou, O King divine' by F Bland Tucker (1895–1984)

29 EVENTIDE

Abide with me; fast falls the eventide

Adapted from a choir arrangement
by David Willcocks

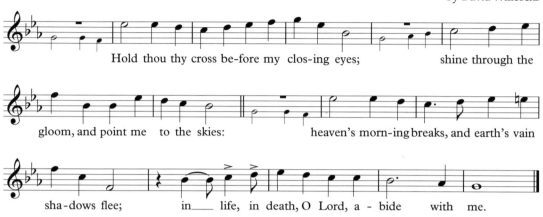

Hold thou thy cross be-fore my clos-ing eyes; shine through the gloom, and point me to the skies: heaven's morn-ing breaks, and earth's vain sha-dows flee; in life, in death, O Lord, a - bide with me.

Eventide by William Henry Monk (1823–89)
Descant by David Willcocks (b. 1919) © 1976 Oxford University Press
Text: 'Abide with me; fast falls the eventide' by Henry Francis Lyte (1793–1847)

30 FAITHFUL ONE

Faithful one, so unchanging

Descant by David Thorne

With feeling

Melody

Faith - ful one, so un - chang - ing; age - less one, you're my rock of peace. Lord of all, I de- -pend on you, I call out to you a-gain and a - gain, I call out to you a-gain and a - gain. You are my rock in times of trou - ble, you lift me up

Melody and words by Brian Doerksen (b. 1965)
Descant by David Thorne (b. 1950)
© 1989 Vineyard Songs & ION Publishing. Administered by Song Solutions CopyCare <www.songsolutions.org>

when I fall down, all through the storm your love, your love is the an - chor, my hope, my hope in you a - lone.

31a & b FAITHFULNESS (in E♭ and D)

Great is thy faithfulness, O God my Father

Descant by Paul Leddington Wright
and Robert Prizeman

31a in E♭

Great, O great, morn-ing by morn-ing new mer-cies I see; all I have need-ed thy hand hath pro - vi-ded, great is thy faith-ful-ness, Lord, un-to me.

31b in D

Great, O great, morn-ing by morn-ing new mer-cies I see; all I have need-ed thy hand hath pro - vi-ded, great is thy faith-ful-ness, Lord, un-to me.

Faithfulness (or *Great is thy faithfulness*) by William M Runyan (1870–1957). Descant by Paul Leddington Wright (b. 1951) and Robert Prizeman (b. 1952). Text: 'Great is thy faithfulness, O God my Father' by Thomas Chisholm (1866–1960).

32 FATHER, WE ADORE YOU

Father, we adore you

Descant by William Llewellyn

Al - le - lu - ia, al - le - lu - ia! Al - le - lu - ia, al - le - lu - ia! Al - le - lu - ia, al - le - lu - ia!

Melody and words by Terrye Coelho (b. 1952)
Descant by William Llewellyn (b. 1925)

33 FATHER, WE LOVE YOU

Father, we love you, we worship and adore you

Descant by William Llewellyn

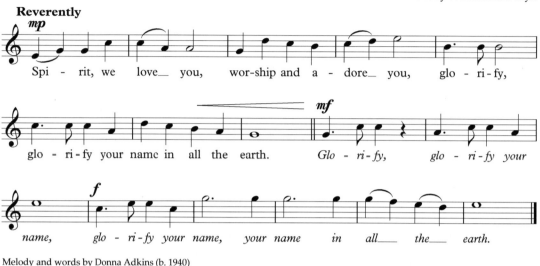

Reverently
mp

Spi - rit, we love_ you, wor-ship and a - dore_ you, glo - ri - fy,

glo - ri - fy your name in all the earth. *Glo - ri - fy*, *glo - ri - fy your*

mf

name, glo - ri - fy your name, your name in all_ the_ earth.

f

Melody and words by Donna Adkins (b. 1940)
Descant by William Llewellyn (b. 1925)
© 1976/1981 CCCM Music & Maranatha! Music / Universal Music (Print/Sync rights in the UK/Eire only by
Small Stone Media BV, Holland). Administered by Song Solutions Daybreak <www.songsolutions.org>

34 FOREST GREEN

O little town of Bethlehem

Descant by Thomas Armstrong

O ho - ly_ Child of Beth - le - hem, des - cend to us, we pray;

Cast out our_ sin, and en - ter in, be born in us to - day.

We_ hear the Christ-mas an - gels the great glad ti - dings tell:

O come to_ us, a - bide with us, our Lord Em - ma - nu - el!

Forest Green—English traditional melody collected, adapted, and arranged by Ralph Vaughan Williams (1872–1958) from
The English Hymnal. Reproduced by permission of Oxford University Press. All rights reserved
Descant by Thomas Armstrong (1898–1994) © The Royal School of Church Music. Used by permission
Text: 'O little town of Bethlehem' by Phillips Brooks (1835–93)

35a & b GERONTIUS (in A♭ and G)

Praise to the Holiest in the height

Descant by Robert Gower

35a in A♭

Praise to the Ho - liest in the height, and in the depth_ be praise;

in all his words most won - der - ful, most sure_ in all his ways!

35b in G

Praise to the Ho - liest in the height, and in the depth_ be praise;

in all his words most won - der - ful, most sure_ in all his ways!

Gerontius by John Bacchus Dykes (1823–76)
Descant by Robert Gower (b. 1952) © 2012 Oxford University Press
Text: 'Praise to the Holiest in the height' by John Henry Newman (1801–90)

36 GOD REST YOU MERRY

God rest you merry, gentlemen

Descant by Christopher Robinson

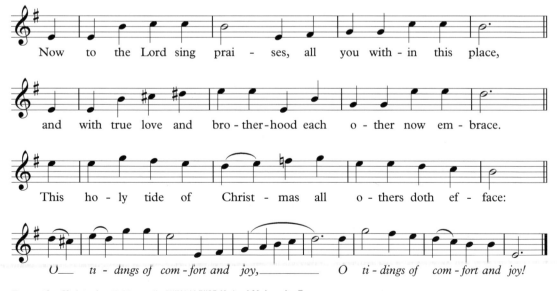

Now to the Lord sing prai - ses, all you with - in this place,

and with true love and bro - ther-hood each o - ther now em - brace.

This ho - ly tide of Christ - mas all o - thers doth ef - face:

O_ ti - dings of com - fort and joy,_ O ti - dings of com - fort and joy!

Descant by Christopher Robinson (b. 1936) © 2012 Oxford University Press
Tune and words—English traditional carol

37 GUITING POWER

Christ triumphant, ever reigning

Descant by John Barnard

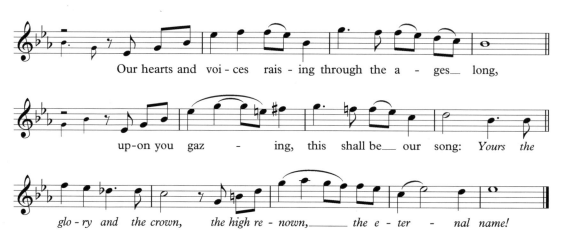

Our hearts and voi - ces rais - ing through the a - ges__ long,
up-on you gaz - ing, this shall be__ our song: *Yours the*
glo - ry and the crown, the high re - nown,_____ the e - ter - nal name!

Hymn tune and descant by John Barnard (b. 1948) © John Barnard/Jubilate Hymns
Text: 'Christ triumphant, ever reigning' by Michael Saward (b. 1932) © Michael Saward/Jubilate Hymns
Administered by the Jubilate Group, 4 Thorpe Park Road, Torquay TQ2 6RX. <copyrightmanager@jubilate.co.uk>
Used by permission

38 HANOVER

O worship the King, all glorious above
The kingdom of God is justice and joy

Descant by Alan Gray

O mea - sure - less might, in - eff - a - ble__ love, while
God's king - dom is come, the gift and the__ goal, in

an - gels de - light to hymn thee__ a - bove,
Je - sus be - gun, in hea - ven made whole;

thy hum - bler cre - a - tion, though fee - ble their lays, with__
the heirs of the king - dom shall__ ans - wer his call, and__

true__ a - do - ra - tion shall sing to__ thy praise.
all__ things cry__ 'Glo - ry!' to God all__ in all.

Hanover probably by William Croft (1678–1727)
Descant by Alan Gray (1855–1935)
First text: 'O worship the King, all glorious above' by Robert Grant (1780–1838)
Second text: 'The kingdom of God is justice and joy' by Bryn Rees (1911–83) © Alexander Scott

39 HELMSLEY

Lo, he comes with clouds descending

Descant by John Rutter

Yea, A - men! let all a - dore thee, high___ on thine e - ter - nal___ throne; Sa - viour, take the power and glo - ry: claim___ the king-dom for thine own:___ O___come quick- ly, O___come quick- ly,
_Al - le - lu - ia, al - le - lu - ia,_

O___ come quick- ly! Al - le - lu - ia!___ Come, Lord, come!
_al - le - lu - ia! Thou shalt reign, and___ thou___ a - lone._
_(Ev - er - last - ing___ God, come down!)_

Helmsley included in John Wesley's *Select Hymns* 1765. Descant by John Rutter (b. 1945) © 2000 Collegium Music Publications
Text: 'Lo, he comes with clouds descending' by John Cennick (1718–55) and Charles Wesley (1707–88)

40 HIGHWOOD

'Glory to God!' all heaven with joy is ringing
O Lord of every shining constellation
O perfect Love, all human thought transcending

Descant by Robert Gower

No crib or cra - dle is con - ceal - ing___ Je - sus our Lord in
Great Lord,___ sha - ping and re - new - ing,___ you made us more than
The joy which bright-ens earth-ly sor - row;___ grant them the peace which

that far - dis-tant shrine, Christ at___ each Eu - char - ist is___ still___ re -
na - ture's sons to be; you help_ us tread, with grace our_ souls___ en -
calms all earth-ly strife, and to_ life's day the_ glo - rious un - known

-veal - ing___ his ve - ry self in forms of bread___ and wine.
-du - ing,___ the road to life and im - mor - ta - li - ty.
mor - row___ that dawns up - on e - ter - nal love___ and life.

Highwood by Richard R Terry (1865–1938). Descant by Robert Gower (b. 1952) © 2012 Oxford University Press
First text: '"Glory to God!" all heaven with joy is ringing' by John E Bowers (b. 1923) © John E Bowers
Second text: 'O Lord of every shining constellation' by Albert F Bayly (1901–84) © Oxford University Press
Third text: 'O perfect Love, all human thought transcending' by Dorothy F Gurney (1858–1932)

41a & b HOLY IS THE LORD (in A and G)

Holy, holy, holy is the Lord

Descant by Ashley Grote

41a in A

41b in G

Music and words anon. (words based on Revelation 4: 8 & 11). Descant by Ashley Grote (b. 1982) © 2012 Oxford University Press

42 HYFRYDOL

Alleluia, sing to Jesus

Ye that know the Lord is gracious

Descant by John Scott

Hyfrydol by Rowland Hugh Prichard (1811–87). Descant by John Scott (b. 1956) © 2001 Banks Music Publications. Reproduced by permission. First text: 'Alleluia, sing to Jesus' by William Chatterton Dix (1837–98). Second text: 'Ye that know the Lord is gracious' by Cyril A Alington (1872–1955) © Hymns Ancient & Modern Ltd

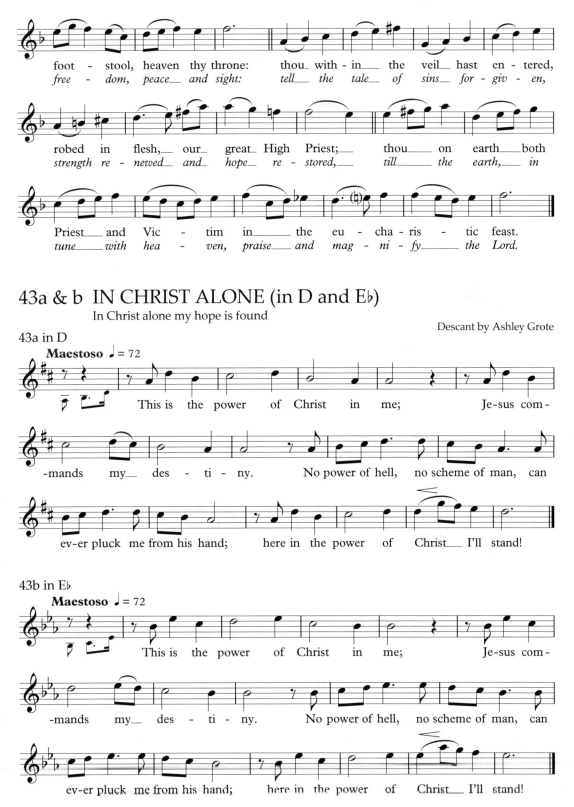

foot - stool, heaven thy throne: thou within the veil hast en - tered,
free - dom, peace and sight: tell the tale of sins for - giv - en,

robed in flesh, our great High Priest; thou on earth both
strength re - newed and hope re - stored, till the earth, in

Priest and Vic - tim in the eu - cha - ris - tic feast.
tune with hea - ven, praise and mag - ni - fy the Lord.

43a & b IN CHRIST ALONE (in D and E♭)

In Christ alone my hope is found

Descant by Ashley Grote

43a in D

Maestoso ♩ = 72

This is the power of Christ in me; Je-sus com-

-mands my des - ti - ny. No power of hell, no scheme of man, can

ev-er pluck me from his hand; here in the power of Christ I'll stand!

43b in E♭

Maestoso ♩ = 72

This is the power of Christ in me; Je-sus com-

-mands my des - ti - ny. No power of hell, no scheme of man, can

ev-er pluck me from his hand; here in the power of Christ I'll stand!

Melody and words by Stuart Townend (b. 1963) and Keith Getty (b. 1974). Descant by Ashley Grote (b. 1982)
© 2001 Thankyou Music / Administered by worshiptogether.com Songs, excluding UK & Europe, administered by
kingswaysongs, a division of David C Cook <tym@kingsway.co.uk> Used by permission

44a & b IRBY (in F and G)
Once in royal David's city

Descant by Benjamin Lamb

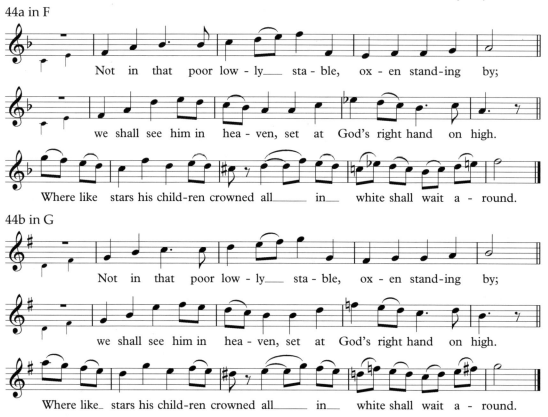

44a in F

Not in that poor low - ly__ sta - ble, ox - en stand-ing by;

we shall see him in hea - ven, set at God's right hand on high.

Where like stars his child-ren crowned all____ in__ white shall wait a - round.

44b in G

Not in that poor low - ly__ sta - ble, ox - en stand-ing by;

we shall see him in hea - ven, set at God's right hand on high.

Where like_ stars his child-ren crowned all____ in__ white shall wait a - round.

Irby by Henry Gauntlett (1805–76)
Descant by Benjamin Lamb (b. 1974) © 2012 Oxford University Press
Text: 'Once in royal David's city' by Cecil Frances Alexander (1818–95)

45a JESUS IS LORD (in G)
Jesus is Lord! Creation's voice proclaims it

Descant by James Whitbourn

*Ah_____ ah_____

ah_____ ah_____

Je - sus is Lord, Je - sus is Lord! Praise him, praise him for Je - sus is Lord!

* 'Ah' should be pronounced as in 'u' in under.

Melody and words by David Mansell (b. 1936). Descant by James Whitbourn (b. 1963). © 1982 Authentic Publishing administered by kingswaysongs, a division of David C Cook <tym@kingsway.co.uk> Used by permission

45b JESUS IS LORD (in A♭)

Jesus is Lord! Creation's voice proclaims it

Descant by James Whitbourn

*Ah_____ ah_____

ah_____ ah_____

Je-sus is Lord, Je-sus is Lord! Praise him, praise him for Je-sus is Lord!

* 'Ah' should be pronounced as in 'u' in under.

46a LASST UNS ERFREUEN (in D)

All creatures of our God and King

Ye watchers and ye holy ones

Descant by Christopher Gower

Let all things their cre-a-tor bless,___ and wor-ship him. O___
O friends, in glad-ness let us sing,___ su - per - nal an-thems, al -

praise him,___ al-le-lu - ia! Praise the Fa - ther,
- le-lu - ia,___ al-le-lu - ia! God the Fa - ther,

praise the Son, Spi-rit,_Three in One:___ O___ praise him, O___
God the Son, Spi-rit,_Three in One:___ Al - le-lu - ia, al-le-

praise him, Al-le-lu - ia, al-le-lu - ia, al-le-lu - - ia!
-lu - ia, al-le-lu - ia, al-le-lu - ia, al-le-lu - - ia!

46b LASST UNS ERFREUEN (in E♭)

All creatures of our God and King

Ye watchers and ye holy ones

Descant by Christopher Gower

Let all things their cre-a-tor bless,___ and wor-ship him. O
O friends, in glad-ness let us sing,___ su - per-nal an-thems, al -

_____ praise him,_ al-le-lu - ia! Praise the Fa - ther,
- le-lu - ia,_ al-le-lu - ia! God the Fa - ther,

praise the Son, Spi-rit,_Three in One:_____ O_____ praise him, O__
God the Son, Spi-rit,_Three in One:_____ Al-le - lu - ia, al-le-

praise_him, Al-le-lu - ia, al-le-lu - ia, al-le-lu - - ia!
-lu - ia, al-le-lu - ia, al-le-lu - ia, al-le-lu - - ia!

47a & b LAUDES DOMINI (in C and B♭)

When morning gilds the skies

Descant by Reginald Thatcher

47a in C

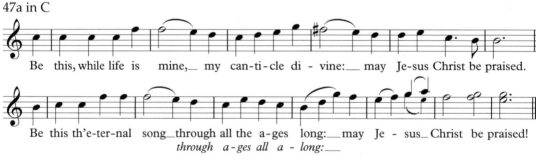

Be this, while life is mine,_ my can-ti-cle di - vine:_ may Je-sus Christ be praised.

Be this th'e-ter-nal song_through all the a-ges long:_may Je - sus_Christ be praised!
through a-ges all a - long:_

47b in B♭

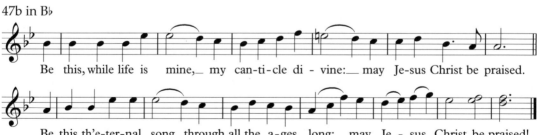

Be this, while life is mine,_ my can-ti-cle di - vine:_ may Je-sus Christ be praised.

Be this th'e-ter-nal song_through all the a-ges long:_may Je - sus_Christ be praised!
through a-ges all a - long:_

48 LAUDS
There's a spirit in the air

Descant by John Wilson

Praise___ the love,___ praise___ the love!___

Al - le - lu - ia, al - - le - lu - ia!___

Hymn tune and descant by John Wilson (1905–92) © The Estate of John Wilson. Administered by Oxford University Press
Text: 'There's a spirit in the air' by Brian Wren (b. 1936) © 1969, 1995 Stainer & Bell Ltd, 23 Gruneisen Road, London N3 1DZ

49 LAUS DEO (REDHEAD No. 46)
Bright the vision that delighted

Descant from *Hymns Ancient & Modern Revised*
probably by Sydney H Nicholson

'Lord, thy glo - ry fills the__ hea - ven; earth is with its full - ness stored;

un - to__ thee be glo - ry giv - en, ho - ly, ho - ly, ho - ly, Lord.'

Laus Deo by Richard Redhead (1820–1901). Descant from *Hymns Ancient & Modern Revised* probably by Sydney H Nicholson
(1875–1947) © Hymns Ancient & Modern Ltd. Used by permission.
Text: 'Bright the vision that delighted' by Richard Mant (1776–1848)

50a LOBE DEN HERREN (PRAXIS PIETATIS) (in F)
Praise to the Lord, the Almighty, the King of creation

Descant by Harrison Oxley

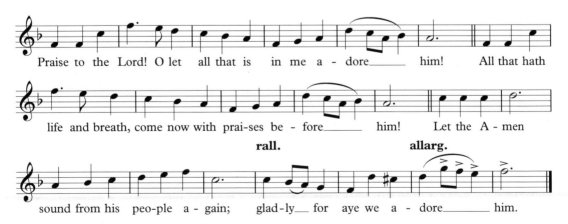

Praise to the Lord! O let all that is in me a - dore___ him! All that hath

life and breath, come now with prai - ses be - fore___ him! Let the A - men

rall. *allarg.*

sound from his peo - ple a - gain; glad - ly__ for aye we a - dore___ him.

Lobe den Herren—17th-century German melody
Descant by Harrison Oxley (1933–2009) © 1988 The Royal School of Church Music. Used by permission
Text: 'Praise to the Lord, the Almighty' tr. by Catherine Winkworth (1827–78) from Joachim Neander (1650–80)

50b LOBE DEN HERREN (PRAXIS PIETATIS) (in G)

Praise to the Lord, the Almighty, the King of creation

Descant by Harrison Oxley

Praise to the Lord! O let all that is in me a - dore____ him! All that hath

life and breath, come now with prai-ses be - fore____ him! Let the A - men

sound from his peo-ple a - gain; glad-ly__ for aye we a - dore____ him.

Lobe den Herren—17th-century German melody
Descant by Harrison Oxley (1933–2009) © 1988 The Royal School of Church Music. Used by permission
Text: 'Praise to the Lord, the Almighty' tr. by Catherine Winkworth (1827–78) from Joachim Neander (1650–80)

51 LORD OF THE YEARS

Lord, for the years your love has kept and guided

Descant by John Barnard

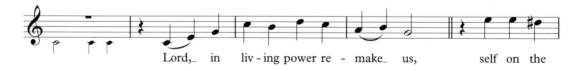

Lord,__ in liv-ing power re - make_ us, self on the

cross and__ Christ up-on the throne; for__ the fu - ture

take__ us, Lord of our lives,__ to__ live for Christ a - lone.

Lord of the years by Michael Baughen (b. 1930). Music © Michael Baughen / Jubilate Hymns; descant by John Barnard (b. 1948)
© John Barnard / Jubilate Hymns. Administered by The Jubilate Group, 4 Thorne Park Road, Torquay TQ2 6RX
<copyrightmanager@jubilate.co.uk> Used by permission
Text: 'Lord, for the years your love has kept and guided' by Timothy Dudley-Smith (b. 1926) © Timothy Dudley-Smith in Europe
and Africa. © Hope Publishing Company in the United States of America and the rest of the world. Reproduced by permission of
Oxford University Press. All rights reserved

52 LUCKINGTON
Let all the world in every corner sing

Descant by William Mathias

Let all the world in ev-ery cor-ner sing, my God and King.

The church with psalms must shout, no door can keep them out;

but a-bove all the heart must bear the long-est part.

Allargando

Let all the world in ev-ery cor-ner sing, my God and King.

Luckington by Basil Harwood (1859–1949) © The Estate of Basil Harwood
Descant by William Mathias (1934–92) from his anthem *Let all the world in every corner sing* © 1987 Oxford University Press
Text: 'Let all the world in every corner sing' by George Herbert (1593–1633)

53 LUX EOI
Alleluia, alleluia! Hearts to heaven and voices raise

Descant by Richard Lloyd

Al - le-lu-ia, al - le-lu - ia! Glo-ry be to God on high;

Al - le-lu-ia to the Sa-viour, who has gained the vic-to-ry;
to the Fa-ther, and the Sa-viour,

Al - le-lu-ia to the Spi-rit, fount of love and sanc-ti-ty:
glo-ry to the Ho-ly Spi-rit,

Al - le - lu - ia! to the Tri-une Ma-je-sty.

Lux eoi by Arthur Sullivan (1842–1900)
Descant by Richard Lloyd (b. 1933) © 1990 Kevin Mayhew Ltd. Reproduced by permission; Licence Nr 217011/1
<www.kevinmayhew.com>
Text: 'Alleluia, alleluia! Hearts to heaven and voices raise' by Christopher Wordsworth (1807–85)

54a MACCABAEUS (in E♭)

Thine be the glory, risen, conquering Son

Descant by Malcolm Archer

No more we doubt thee, glo - rious Prince of Life;___

life___ is___ naught with - out___ thee: aid___ us in our strife;

make us___ more than con - querors through thy death-less___ love; bring___ us

safe___ through Jor - dan___ to thy home a - bove:

Thine be the glo - ry, ri - sen, con-quering Son, end-less is___ the___

vic - tory,___ the___ vic - tory thou___ o'er death hast won.

Maccabaeus by G F Handel (1685–1759). Descant by Malcolm Archer (b. 1952) © 1990 Kevin Mayhew Ltd.
Reproduced by permission; Licence Nr 217011/1 <www.kevinmayhew.com>
Text: 'Thine be the glory, risen, conquering Son' by Richard Hoyle (1875–1939) from Edmond Budry (1854–1932)

54b MACCABAEUS (in D)

Thine be the glory, risen, conquering Son

Descant by Malcolm Archer

No more we doubt thee, glo - rious Prince of Life;____

life____ is____ naught with - out____ thee: aid__ us in our strife;

make us__ more than con - querors through thy death-less__ love; bring__ us

safe_____ through Jor - dan__ to thy home a - bove:

Thine be the glo - ry, ri - sen, con-quering Son, end-less is__ the__

vic - tory,_____ the__ vic - tory thou__ o'er death hast won.

55a & b MELCOMBE (in E♭ and D)

New every morning is the love

Descant by Alan Gray

55a in E♭

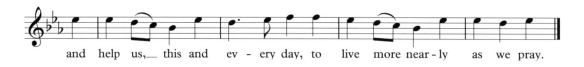

On - ly, O__ Lord, in thy dear love fit us for per - fect rest a - bove;

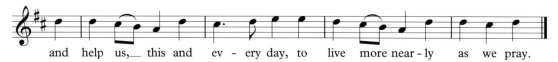

and help us,__ this and ev - ery day, to live more near - ly as we pray.

55b in D

On - ly, O__ Lord, in thy dear love fit us for per - fect rest a - bove;

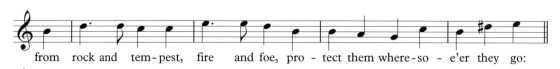

and help us,__ this and ev - ery day, to live more near - ly as we pray.

Melcombe by Samuel Webbe the elder (1740–1816)
Descant by Alan Gray (1855–1935)
Text: 'New every morning is the love' by John Keble (1792–1866)

56 MELITA

Eternal Father, strong to save

Descant by Alan Gray

O Tri - ni - ty of love and__ power, our breth-ren shield in__ dan - ger's hour;

from rock and tem- pest, fire and foe, pro - tect them where-so - e'er they go:

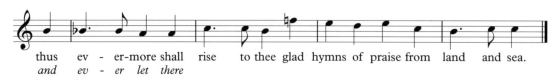

thus ev - er-more shall rise to thee glad hymns of praise from land and sea.
and ev - er let there

Melita by John Bacchus Dykes (1823–76)
Descant by Alan Gray (1855–1935)
Text: 'Eternal Father, strong to save' by William Whiting (1825–78)

57a & b MENDELSSOHN (BETHLEHEM) (in F and G)

Hark! the herald-angels sing

Descant by David Willcocks

57a in F

Hail, the heaven-born Prince of Peace! Hail, the Sun of Right-eous-ness!

Light and life to all he brings, risen with heal-ing in his wings.

Mild he lays his glo-ry by, born that man no more may die,

born to raise the sons of earth, born to give them se-cond birth.

ff

Hark! the he-rald-an-gels sing glo-ry to the new-born King.

57b in G

Hail, the heaven-born Prince of Peace! Hail, the Sun of Right-eous-ness!

Light and life to all he brings, risen with heal-ing in his wings.

Mild he lays his glo-ry by, born that man no more may die,

born to raise the sons of earth, born to give them se-cond birth.

ff

Hark! the he-rald-an-gels sing glo-ry to the new-born King.

Mendelssohn—from a chorus in *Festgesang* by Felix Mendelssohn (1809–47)
Descant by David Willcocks (b. 1919) © 1961 Oxford University Press
Text: 'Hark! the herald-angels sing' by Charles Wesley (1707–88)

58a & b MERTON (in F and E)

Hark, a thrilling voice is sounding

Jesus calls us: o'er the tumult

Descant by Alan Gray

58a in F

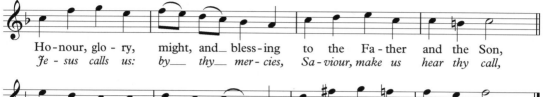

Ho-nour, glo - ry, might, and bless-ing to the Fa - ther and the Son,
Je - sus calls us: by thy mer - cies, Sa - viour, make us hear thy call,

with the ev - er - last-ing Spi - rit, while e - ter - nal a - ges run.
give our hearts to thine o - be - dience, serve and love thee best of all.

58b in E

Ho-nour, glo - ry, might, and bless-ing to the Fa - ther and the Son,
Je - sus calls us: by thy mer - cies, Sa - viour, make us hear thy call,

with the ev - er - last-ing Spi - rit, while e - ter - nal a - ges run.
give our hearts to thine o - be - dience, serve and love thee best of all.

Merton by William Henry Monk (1823–89)
Descant by Alan Gray (1855–1935)
First text: 'Hark, a thrilling voice is sounding' translated by Edward Caswall (1814–78) from sixth-century Latin
Second text: 'Jesus calls us: o'er the tumult' by Cecil Frances Alexander (1818–95)

59 MILES LANE

All hail the power of Jesu's name

Descant by Alan Gray

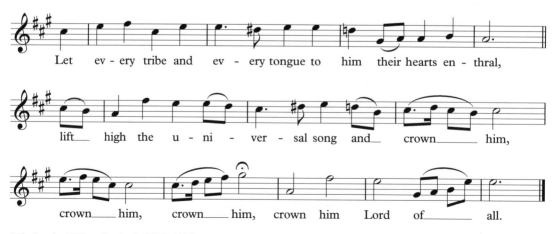

Let ev - ery tribe and ev - ery tongue to him their hearts en - thral,

lift high the u - ni - ver - sal song and crown him,

crown him, crown him, crown him Lord of all.

Miles Lane by William Shrubsole (?1760–1806)
Descant by Alan Gray (1855–1935)
Text: 'All hail the power of Jesu's name' by Edward Perronet (1721–92) and John Rippon (1751–1836)

60 MONKLAND

Let us, with a gladsome mind
Praise, O praise our God and King

Descant by John Wilson

Let us praise the Lord,_____ Al - - le - lu - ia!
Glo - ry let__ us sing,_____ Al - - le - lu - ia!__

_____ For his__ mer - cies ay en - dure, Al - le - lu - ia!
_____ Glo - ry__ to__ the Three in One, Al - le - lu - ia!

Monkland by John Antes (1740–1811)
Descant by John Wilson (1905–92) © The Estate of John Wilson. Administered by Oxford University Press
First text: 'Let us, with a gladsome mind' by John Milton (1608–74)
Second text: 'Praise, O praise our God and King' by Henry Williams Baker (1821–77)

61 MONKS GATE

He who would valiant be
Who would true valour see

Descant by Cyril Winn

Since,__ Lord, thou dost__ de - fend us with thy spi - rit,
Hob - gob - lin nor__ foul fiend can daunt his spi - rit;

we_____ know we at the end shall life__ in - he - rit.
he_____ knows he at the end shall life__ in - he - rit.

Then__ fan - cies flee a - way! I'll fear not what men__ say:
Then,__ fan - cies, fly a - way! He'll fear not what men__ say;

I'll la - bour night__ and day to be__ a__ pil - grim.
he'll la - bour night__ and day to be__ a__ pil - grim.

Monks Gate—English traditional melody collected, adapted, and arranged by Ralph Vaughan Williams (1872–1958) from
The English Hymnal Reproduced by permission of Oxford University Press. All rights reserved
Descant by Cyril Winn (1884–1973) © 1961 Oxford University Press
First text: 'He who would valiant be' by John Bunyan (1628–88) and Percy Dearmer (1867–1936)
Second text: 'Who would true valour see' by John Bunyan (1628–88)

62 MORNING HYMN

Awake, my soul, and with the sun

Descant by David Willcocks

Praise__ God, from whom all bless - ings__ flow, praise__

him, all crea - tures__ here be - low, praise him a - bove, an -
ye

-gel - ic__ host, praise Fa - ther, Son, and Ho - ly Ghost.
heaven - ly__ host,

Morning Hymn by François H Barthélémon (1741–1808)
Descant by David Willcocks (b. 1919) © 2012 Oxford University Press
Text: 'Awake, my soul, and with the sun' by Thomas Ken (1637–1711)

63 MOSCOW

Thou whose almighty word

Descant by Alan Gray

Ho - ly and bless - ed Three, glo - ri - ous Tri - ni - ty,
Bless - ed and ho - ly Three,

Wis - dom, Love, Might; bound-less as o - cean's tide, roll - ing in

full - est pride, through the earth far, let__ there be light!

Moscow by Felice de Giardini (1716–96)
Descant by Alan Gray (1855–1935)
Text: 'Thou whose almighty word' by John Marriott (1780–1825)

64 NEANDER (UNSER HERRSCHER)

Come, ye faithful, raise the anthem

Descant from *Hymns Ancient & Modern Revised*
probably by Sydney H Nicholson

Laud and ho-nour to the Fa-ther, laud and ho-nour to the Son,

laud and ho-nour to the Spi-rit, ev-er Three and ev-er One,

con-sub-stan-tial, co-e-ter-nal, while un-end-ing a-ges run.

Neander by Joachim Neander (1650–80)
Descant from *Hymns Ancient & Modern Revised* probably by Sydney H Nicholson (1875–1947) © Hymns Ancient & Modern Ltd.
Used by permission
Text: 'Come, ye faithful, raise the anthem'—final verse by John Mason Neale (1818–66)

65 NICAEA

Holy, holy, holy! Lord God Almighty

Descant by James Vivian

Ho-ly, ho-ly! Lord God Al-might-y!

all thy works shall praise thy name in earth and sky and sea;

ho-ly, ho-ly, Lord God Al-might-y!___

God___ in three per-sons, bless-ed Tri-ni-ty!

Nicaea by John Bacchus Dykes (1823–76)
Descant by James Vivian (b. 1974) © 2012 Oxford University Press
Text: 'Holy, holy, holy! Lord God Almighty' by Reginald Heber (1783–1826)

42

66 NOEL
It came upon the midnight clear

Descant by David Willcocks

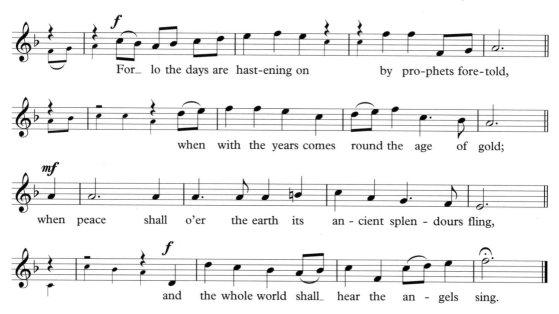

For lo the days are hast-ening on by pro-phets fore-told,

when with the years comes round the age of gold;

when peace shall o'er the earth its an-cient splen-dours fling,

and the whole world shall hear the an-gels sing.

Noel—English traditional melody adapted by Arthur Sullivan (1842–1900)
Descant by David Willcocks (b. 1919) © 1970 Oxford University Press
Text: 'It came upon the midnight clear' by Edmund Sears (1810–76)

67a NUN DANKET (in F)
Now thank we all our God

Descant by William H Harris

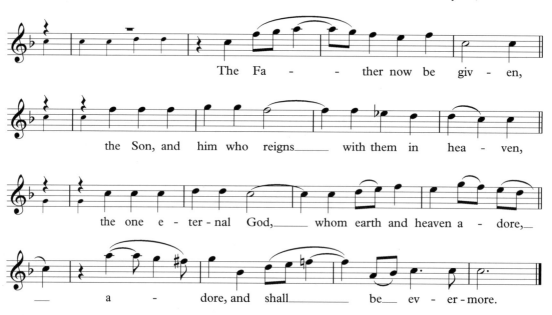

The Fa - - ther now be giv - en,

the Son, and him who reigns with them in hea - ven,

the one e - ter - nal God, whom earth and heaven a - dore,

a - dore, and shall be ev - er - more.

Nun danket probably by Johann Crüger (1598–1662)
Descant by William H Harris (1883–1973) © The Royal School of Church Music. Used by permission
Text: 'Now thank we all our God' translated by Catherine Winkworth (1827–78) from Martin Rinkart (1586–1649)

67b NUN DANKET (in E♭)

Now thank we all our God

Descant by William H Harris

The Fa - - ther now be giv - en,
the Son, and him who reigns___ with them in hea - ven,
the one e - ter - nal God,___ whom earth and heaven a - dore,___
___ a - dore, and shall___ be___ ev - er - more.

Nun danket probably by Johann Crüger (1598–1662)
Descant by William H Harris (1883–1973) © The Royal School of Church Music. Used by permission
Text: 'Now thank we all our God' translated by Catherine Winkworth (1827–78) from Martin Rinkart (1586–1649)

68 ORIEL

To the name of our salvation

Descant by Alan Gray

2. Je - sus is the name we trea - sure, name be - yond what words can tell;
6. There-fore we in love a - dor - ing this most bless - ed name re - vere,

name of glad - ness, name of plea - sure, ear___ and___ heart de - light - ing well;
ho - ly Je - su, thee im - plor - ing so___ to___ write it in us here,

name of sweet - ness, pass - ing mea - sure, sav - ing us from sin and hell,
that here - af - ter, heaven - ward soar - ing, we may sing with an - gels there.

Oriel from Caspar Ett's *Cantica Sacra* 1840
Descant by Alan Gray (1855–1935)
Text: 'To the name of our salvation' translated by John Mason Neale (1818–66) from 15th-century Latin

69 PRAISE, MY SOUL (LAUDA ANIMA)

Praise, my soul, the King of heaven

Descant by Alan Gray

An - gels, help us to a - dore him;— ye be - hold him face to face;

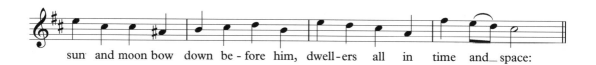

sun and moon bow down be - fore him, dwell-ers all in time and— space:

or Praise him, praise___ him,

Al - le - lu - ia, al - le - lu - ia, praise with us the God of grace.

Praise, my soul by John Goss (1800–80)
Descant by Alan Gray (1855–1935)
Text: 'Praise, my soul, the King of heaven' by Henry Francis Lyte (1793–1847)

70 PUER NOBIS NASCITUR

Come, thou Redeemer of the earth

Descant by John Scott

O Je - su, vir - gin born,___ to thee e - ter - nal

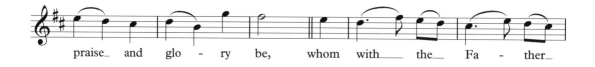

praise— and glo - ry be, whom with— the— Fa - ther—

we— a - dore and Ho - ly Spi - rit, ev - er - more.

Puer nobis nascitur — medieval German carol melody adapted by Michael Praetorius (1571–1621)
Descant by John Scott (b. 1956) © 2001 Banks Music Publications. Reproduced by permission
Text: 'Come, thou Redeemer of the earth' translated by John Mason Neale (1818–66) from St Ambrose (c.340–97)

71 QUAM DILECTA
We love the place, O God

Descant by John Henderson

We love to sing be - low for mer - cies free - ly given;

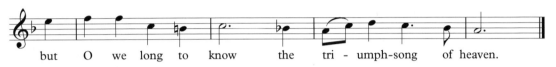

but O we long to know the tri - umph-song of heaven.

Quam dilecta by Henry Jenner (1820–98)
Descant by John Henderson (b. 1945) © 2012 Oxford University Press
Text: 'We love the place, O God' — final verses by Henry Williams Baker (1821–77)

72 REGENT SQUARE
Light's abode, celestial Salem

Descant by David Thorne

Laud and ho - nour to the Fa - ther, laud and ho - nour to the Son,

laud and ho - nour to the— Spi - rit, ev - er Three and— ev - er One,

con - sub - stan - tial, co - e - ter - nal, while un - end - ing a - ges run.

Regent Square by Henry Smart (1813–79)
Descant by David Thorne (b. 1950) © 2012 Oxford University Press
Text: 'Light's abode, celestial Salem' translated by John Mason Neale (1818–66) from 15th-century Latin

73 REPTON

Dear Lord and Father of mankind

Descant by John Scott

Breathe through our__ de - sire thy cool - ness and thy__

__ balm; let sense be dumb, let flesh re - tire;__ speak

through the__ earth-quake, wind, and fire,__ O__ still small

voice__ of__ calm, O still small voice of calm.

Repton by C Hubert H Parry (1848–1918)
Descant by John Scott (b. 1956) © 2001 Banks Music Publications. Reproduced by permission
Text: 'Dear Lord and Father of mankind' by John Greenleaf Whittier (1807–92)

74a RICHMOND (in F)

City of God, how broad and far

Descant by Edward Bairstow

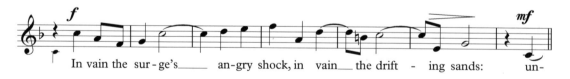

In vain the sur-ge's__ an-gry shock, in vain__ the drift - ing sands: un-

- harmed up - on__ the 'e - ter - nal Rock the 'e - ter - nal Ci - ty stands.

Richmond by Thomas Haweis (1734–1820)
Descant by Edward Bairstow (1874–1946) © 1941 Oxford University Press
Text: 'City of God, how broad and far' by Samuel Johnson (1822–82)

74b RICHMOND (in G)

City of God, how broad and far

Descant by Edward Bairstow

In vain the sur-ge's an-gry shock, in vain the drift-ing sands: un-

-harmed up-on the e-ter-nal Rock the e-ter-nal Ci-ty stands.

Richmond by Thomas Haweis (1734–1820)
Descant by Edward Bairstow (1874–1946) © 1941 Oxford University Press
Text: 'City of God, how broad and far' by Samuel Johnson (1822–82)

75a & b ROCKINGHAM (in D and E♭)

When I survey the wondrous cross
My God, and is thy table spread

Composer of descant is unknown

75a in D

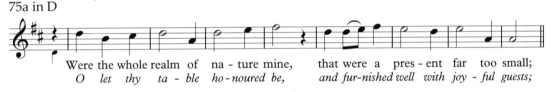

Were the whole realm of na-ture mine, that were a pres-ent far too small;
O let thy ta-ble ho-noured be, and fur-nished well with joy-ful guests;

love so a-maz-ing, so di-vine, de-mands my soul, my life, my all.
and may each soul sal-va-tion see, that here its sa-cred pledg-es tastes.

75b in E♭

Were the whole realm of na-ture mine, that were a pres-ent far too small;
O let thy ta-ble ho-noured be, and fur-nished well with joy-ful guests;

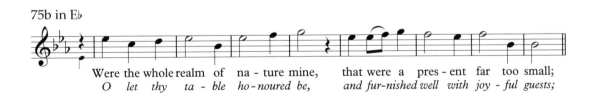

love so a-maz-ing, so di-vine, de-mands my soul, my life, my all.
and may each soul sal-va-tion see, that here its sa-cred pledg-es tastes.

Rockingham adapted by Edward Miller (1735–1807)
First text: 'When I survey the wondrous cross' by Isaac Watts (1674–1748)
Second text: 'My God, and is thy table spread' by Philip Doddridge (1702–51)

76 SAFFRON WALDEN

Just as I am, without one plea

Descant by Simon Lole

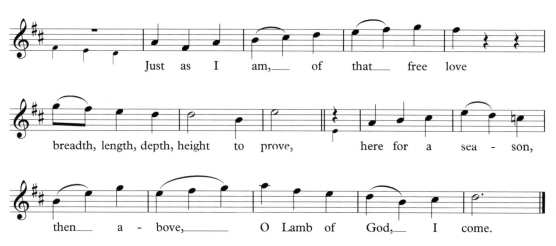

Just as I am,___ of that___ free love breadth, length, depth, height to prove, here for a sea - son, then___ a - bove,_____ O Lamb of God,___ I come.

Saffron Walden by Arthur H Brown (1830–1926)
Descant by Simon Lole (b. 1957) © 2012 Oxford University Press
Text: 'Just as I am, without one plea' by Charlotte Elliott (1789–1871)

77a & b ST ALBINUS (in C and B♭)

Jesus lives! thy terrors now

Descant by John Henderson

77a in C

Je-sus lives! to him the throne o-ver all the world is___giv - en: may we go where

molto allargando

he___ is___gone, rest and reign with him in___hea - ven. Al - le - lu - ia!

77b in B♭

Je-sus lives! to him the throne o-ver all the world is___giv - en: may we go where

molto allargando

he___ is___gone, rest and reign with him in___hea - ven. Al - le - lu - ia!

St Albinus by Henry J Gauntlett (1805–76)
Descant by John Henderson (b. 1945) © 2012 Oxford University Press
Text: 'Jesus lives! thy terrors now' translated by Frances E Cox (1812–97) from Christian Gellert (1715–69)

78 ST ANNE

O God, our help in ages past

Descant by John Scott

O God, our_ help in_ a - ges past, our hope for years to come, be_

thou our_ guard while trou - bles_ last, and_ our e - ter - nal home!

St Anne probably by William Croft (1678–1727)
Descant by John Scott (b. 1956) © 2012 Oxford University Press
Text: 'O God, our help in ages past' by Isaac Watts (1674–1748)

79a & b ST CLEMENT (in A♭ and G)

The day thou gavest, Lord, is ended

Descant by David Blackwell

79a in A♭

So be it,_ Lord: thy throne shall ne-ver, like earth's proud em - pires pass a - way;

thy king-dom stands, and grows_ for ev - er, till_ all thy crea - tures own thy sway.

79b in G

So be it,_ Lord: thy throne shall ne-ver, like earth's proud em - pires pass a - way;

thy king-dom stands, and grows_ for ev - er, till_ all thy crea - tures own thy sway.

St Clement by Clement C Scholefield (1839–1904)
Descant by David Blackwell (b. 1961) © 2012 Oxford University Press
Text: 'The day thou gavest, Lord, is ended' by John Ellerton (1826–93)

80 ST COLUMBA

The King of love my shepherd is

Descant by Donald Davison

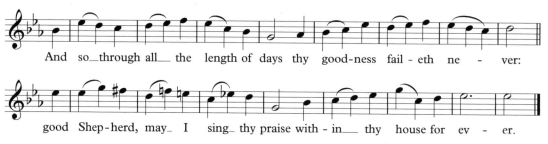

And so through all the length of days thy good-ness fail - eth ne - ver:

good Shep-herd, may I sing thy praise with - in thy house for ev - er.

St Columba—Irish traditional melody
Descant by Donald Davison (b. 1937) © 2000 Oxford University Press
Text: 'The King of love my shepherd is' by Henry Williams Baker (1821–77)

81a & b ST DENIO (in A♭ and G)

Immortal, invisible, God only wise

Descant by Cyril Winn

81a in A♭

Great Fa - ther of glo - ry, pure Fa - ther of light, thine an - gels a -

-dore thee, all veil - ing their sight; all laud we would ren - der: O

help us to see 'tis on - ly the splen-dour of light hi-deth thee.

81b in G

Great Fa - ther of glo - ry, pure Fa - ther of light, thine an - gels a -

-dore thee, all veil - ing their sight; all laud we would ren - der: O

help us to see 'tis on - ly the splen-dour of light hi-deth thee.

St Denio adapted from a Welsh traditional melody
Descant by Cyril Winn (1884–1973) © 1961 Oxford University Press
Text: 'Immortal, invisible, God only wise' by W Chalmers Smith (1824–1908)

82 ST GEORGE'S WINDSOR

Come, ye thankful people, come

Descant by Robert Gower

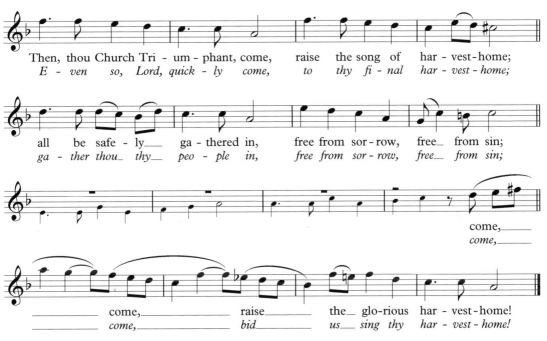

Then, thou Church Tri - um - phant, come, raise the song of har - vest-home;
E - ven so, Lord, quick - ly come, to thy fi - nal har - vest-home;

all be safe - ly___ ga - thered in, free from sor - row, free___ from sin;
ga - ther thou___ thy___ peo - ple in, free from sor - row, free___ from sin;

come,___
come,___

_____ come,_____ raise_____ the___ glo-rious har - vest-home!
_____ come,_____ bid_____ us___ sing thy har - vest-home!

St George's Windsor by George J Elvey (1816–93)
Descant by Robert Gower (b. 1952) © 2012 Oxford University Press
Text: 'Come, ye thankful people, come' by Henry Alford (1810–71)

83 ST HELEN

Lord, enthroned in heavenly splendour

Descant by Christopher Gower

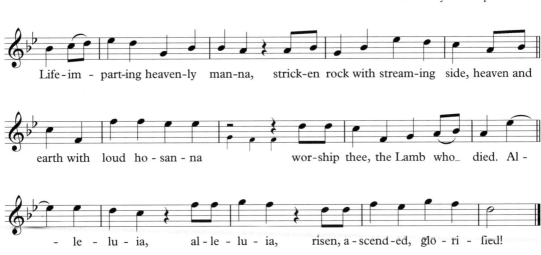

Life - im - part-ing heaven-ly man-na, strick-en rock with stream-ing side, heaven and

earth with loud ho - san - na wor-ship thee, the Lamb who_ died. Al -

- le - lu - ia, al-le-lu - ia, risen, a - scend-ed, glo - ri - fied!

St Helen by George C Martin (1844–1916)
Descant by Christopher Gower (b. 1939) © 1989 Kevin Mayhew Ltd. Reproduced by permission; Licence Nr 217011/1
<www.kevinmayhew.com>
Text: 'Lord, enthroned in heavenly splendour' by George H Bourne (1840–1925)

84 ST MAGNUS

The head that once was crowned with thorns

Descant by John Wilson

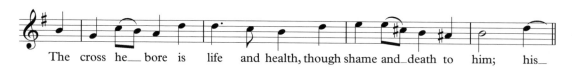

The cross he_ bore is life and health, though shame and_death to him; his_

_ peo-ple's hope, his peo - ple's_wealth, their ev - er - last - ing theme.

St Magnus probably by Jeremiah Clarke (*c.*1674–1707)
Descant by John Wilson (1905–92) © The Estate of John Wilson. Administered by Oxford University Press
Text: 'The head that once was crowned with thorns' by Thomas Kelly (1769–1855)

85 SEEK YE FIRST

Seek ye first the kingdom of God

Descant by William Llewellyn

Al - le - lu - ia, al - le - lu - ia,_

al - le - lu - ia, al - le - lu - ia._

Melody and words by Karen Lafferty (b. 1948)
© 1972 CCCM Music & Maranatha! Music / Universal Music (Print/Sync rights in the UK/Eire only by Small Stone Media BV, Holland). Administered by Song Solutions Daybreak <www.songsolutions.org>

86 SINE NOMINE

For all the saints who from their labours rest

Descant by Cyril Winn

From earth's wide bounds,_ from o - cean's far - thest coast,

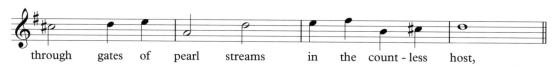

through gates of pearl streams in the count - less host,

Sine Nomine by Ralph Vaughan Williams (1872–1958) from *The English Hymnal.* Reproduced by permission of Oxford University Press. All rights reserved.
Descant by Cyril Winn (1884–1973) © 1961 Oxford University Press.
Text: 'For all the saints who from their labours rest' by W Walsham How (1823–97)

sing - ing to Fa - ther, Son, and Ho - ly Ghost.

Al - le - lu - ia, al - le - lu - ia.

87a & b SING HOSANNA (in E♭ and D)

Give me joy in my heart, keep me praising
Give me oil in my lamp, keep me burning

Traditional descant

87a in E♭

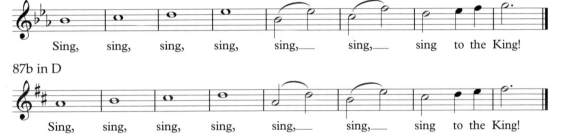

Sing, sing, sing, sing, sing,— sing,— sing to the King!

87b in D

Sing, sing, sing, sing, sing,— sing,— sing to the King!

Music and words from anonymous sources
© 2012 Oxford University Press

88a SLANE

Be thou my vision, O Lord of my heart

Descant by John Wilson

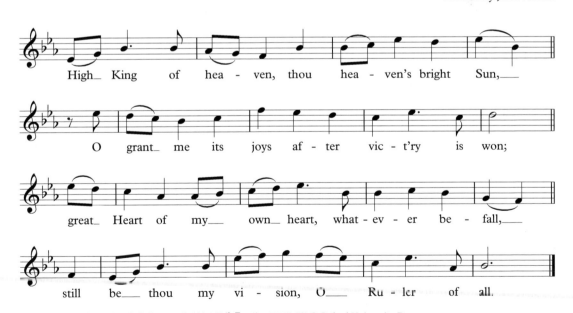

High King of hea - ven, thou hea - ven's bright Sun,

O grant me its joys af - ter vic - t'ry is won;

great Heart of my own heart, what - ev - er be - fall,

still be thou my vi - sion, O Ru - ler of all.

Slane—Irish traditional melody harmonized by Erik Routley (1917–82) © Oxford University Press
Descant by John Wilson (1905–92) © The Estate of John Wilson. Administered by Oxford University Press
Text: 'Be thou my vision, O Lord of my heart'—Irish, versified by Eleanor Hull (1860–1935) from Mary Byrne's translation

88b SLANE

Lord of all hopefulness, Lord of all joy

Descant by David Thorne

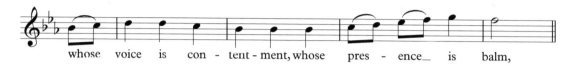

Lord of all gen - tle - ness,__ Lord__ of all__ calm,

whose voice is con - tent - ment, whose pres - ence__ is balm,

be__ there at__ our__ sleep - ing, and give us, we pray,

your peace in our hearts, Lord, at the end of the day.

Slane—Irish traditional melody harmonized by Erik Routley (1917–82) © Oxford University Press
Descant by David Thorne (b. 1950) © 2012 Oxford University Press
Text: 'Lord of all hopefulness, Lord of all joy' by Jan Struther (Joyce Placzek) (1901–53)

89 SONG 34 (ANGELS' SONG)

Forth in thy name, O Lord, I go

Descant by Donald Davison

For thee de - light-ful-ly em-ploy   what-e'er thy boun-teous grace hath given,

and run my__ course with e - ven joy,   and close-ly__ walk with thee__ to__ heaven.

Alternative opening rhythm

For thee de - light - ful-ly em-ploy

Song 34 by Orlando Gibbons (1583–1625)
Descant by Donald Davison (b. 1937) © 2000 Oxford University Press
Text: 'Forth in thy name, O Lord, I go' by Charles Wesley (1707–88)

90a & b STUTTGART (in G and F)

Earth has many a noble city

Come, thou long-expected Jesus

Descant by Antony Baldwin

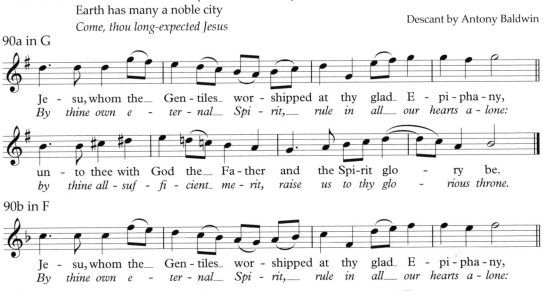

90a in G

Je - su, whom the Gen - tiles wor - shipped at thy glad E - pi - pha - ny,
By thine own e - ter - nal Spi - rit, rule in all our hearts a - lone:

un - to thee with God the Fa - ther and the Spi - rit glo - ry be.
by thine all - suf - fi - cient me - rit, raise us to thy glo - rious throne.

90b in F

Je - su, whom the Gen - tiles wor - shipped at thy glad E - pi - pha - ny,
By thine own e - ter - nal Spi - rit, rule in all our hearts a - lone:

un - to thee with God the Fa - ther and the Spi - rit glo - ry be.
by thine all - suf - fi - cient me - rit, raise us to thy glo - rious throne.

Stuttgart adapted from Witt's *Harmonia Sacra* 1715
Descant by Antony Baldwin (b. 1957) © 2000 Oxford University Press
First text: 'Earth has many a noble city' translated by Edward Caswall (1814–78) from Prudentius (348– *c.*413)
Second text: 'Come, thou long-expected Jesus' by Charles Wesley (1707–88)

91 THE SERVANT KING

From heaven you came, helpless babe

Descant by Ashley Grote

Worshipfully

So let us learn how to serve, and in our lives en-throne

him; each o-ther's needs to pre - fer, for it is Christ we're serv - ing.

This is our God, the Ser-vant King, he calls us now to fol-low him,

to bring our lives as an of-fer-ing of wor-ship to the Ser-vant King.

Music and words by Graham Kendrick (b. 1950)
Descant by Ashley Grote (b. 1982)

92 THORNBURY

Thy hand, O God, has guided

Descant by David Willcocks

Thy mer-cy__ will not fail us, nor__ leave thy work un-done;

with thy right hand to help us, the__ vic-tory shall__ be won;

and__ then by men and an-gels, thy name shall be__ a - dored,__

and this shall be their an - them: one church,__ one faith,__ one faith, one Lord.

Thornbury by Basil Harwood (1859–1949) © The Estate of Basil Harwood
Descant by David Willcocks (b. 1919) © 2012 Oxford University Press
Text: 'Thy hand, O God, has guided' by Edward H Plumptre (1821–91)

93a & b TRURO (in D and C)

Jesus shall reign where'er the sun
Christ is alive! Let Christians sing

Descant by John Wilson

93a in D

Let ev-ery crea-ture rise__ and bring pe-cu-liar ho-nours to our King;
Christ is a-live, and comes to bring good news to this and__ ev-ery age,

an-gels des-cend with songs a - gain,__ and earth re-peat the__ loud A - men.
till earth and__ sky and o - cean ring__ with joy, with jus - tice,__ love, and praise.

93b in C

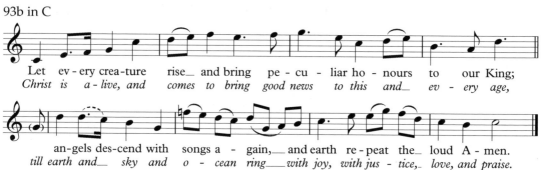

Let ev-ery crea-ture rise__ and bring pe-cu-liar ho-nours to our King;
Christ is a-live, and comes to bring good news to this and__ ev-ery age,

an-gels des-cend with songs a - gain,__ and earth re-peat the__ loud A - men.
till earth and__ sky and o - cean ring__ with joy, with jus - tice,__ love, and praise.

Truro—melody from Thomas Williams's *Psalmodia Evangelica* 1789
Descant by John Wilson (1905–92) © The Estate of John Wilson. Administered by Oxford University Press
First text: 'Jesus shall reign where'er the sun' by Isaac Watts (1674–1748)
Second text: 'Christ is alive! Let Christians sing' by Brian Wren (b. 1936) © 1969, 1995 Stainer & Bell Ltd

94a VENI EMMANUEL (metrical version)

O come, O come, Emmanuel

Descant by Robert Gower

Veni Emmanuel—melody adapted by Thomas Helmore (1811–90)
Descant by Robert Gower (b. 1952) © 2012 Oxford University Press
Text: 'O come, O come, Emmanuel' translated by John Mason Neale (1818–66) from Latin Advent Antiphons

94b VENI EMMANUEL (plainchant version)

O come, O come, Emmanuel

Descant by Robert Gower

Veni Emmanuel—melody adapted by Thomas Helmore (1811–90)
Descant by Robert Gower (b. 1952) © 2012 Oxford University Press
Text: 'O come, O come, Emmanuel' translated by John Mason Neale (1818–66) from Latin Advent Antiphons

95a & b WAREHAM (in B♭ and A)

Jesus, where'er thy people meet
Rejoice, O land, in God thy might

Descant from *Hymns Ancient & Modern Revised*
by Sydney H Nicholson

95a in B♭

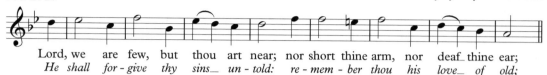

Lord, we are few, but thou art near; nor short thine arm, nor deaf thine ear;
He shall for-give thy sins un-told: re-mem-ber thou his love of old;

O rend the heavens, come quick-ly down, and make a thou-sand hearts thine own!
walk in his way, his word a-dore, and keep his truth for ev - er-more.

95b in A

Lord, we are few, but thou art near; nor short thine arm, nor deaf thine ear;
He shall for-give thy sins un-told: re-mem-ber thou his love of old;

O rend the heavens, come quick-ly down, and make a thou-sand hearts thine own!
walk in his way, his word a-dore, and keep his truth for ev - er-more.

Wareham by William Knapp (1698–1768)
Descant from *Hymns Ancient & Modern Revised* by Sydney H Nicholson (1875–1947) © Hymns Ancient & Modern Ltd. Used by permission.
First text: 'Jesus, where'er thy people meet' by William Cowper (1731–1800)
Second text: 'Rejoice, O land, in God thy might' by Robert Bridges (1844–1930)

96 WAS LEBET

O worship the Lord in the beauty of holiness

Descant by Donald Davison

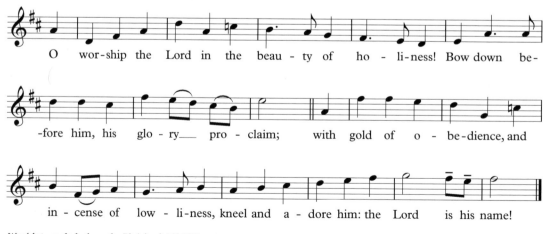

O wor-ship the Lord in the beau - ty of ho - li-ness! Bow down be-

-fore him, his glo - ry pro - claim; with gold of o - be-dience, and

in - cense of low - li-ness, kneel and a - dore him: the Lord is his name!

Was lebet—melody from the *Rheinhardt MS 1754*
Descant by Donald Davison (b. 1937) © 2000 Oxford University Press
Text: 'O worship the Lord in the beauty of holiness' by John S B Monsell (1811–75)

97a & b WESTMINSTER ABBEY (in A♭ and G)

Blessed city, heavenly Salem
Christ is made the sure foundation

Descant by John Rutter

97a in A♭

97b in G

Westminster Abbey adap. Henry Purcell (1659–95)
Descant by John Rutter (b. 1945) © 2000 Collegium Music Publications.
Text: 'Blessed city, heavenly Salem' ('Christ is made the sure foundation') tr. by John Mason Neale (1818–66)

98 WINCHESTER NEW

On Jordan's bank the Baptist's cry

Ride on, ride on in majesty

Descant by Alan Gray

All praise, e - ter - nal Son, to____ thee whose
Ride on, ride on in ma - jes - ty! In

ad - vent____ sets thy peo - ple____ free, whom with the Fa - ther
low - ly____ pomp ride on to____ die; bow thy meek head to

we a - dore, and Ho - ly Ghost for____ ev - er - more.
mor - tal pain, then take, O God,____ thy____ power, and____ reign.

Winchester New adapted from *Musikalisches Hand-Buch* 1690
Descant by Alan Gray (1855–1935)
First text: 'On Jordan's bank the Baptist's cry' tr. by John Chandler (1806–76)
Second text: 'Ride on, ride on in majesty' by Henry H Milman (1791–1868)

99 WINCHESTER OLD

While shepherds watched their flocks by night

Descant by Alan Gray

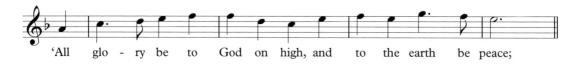

'All glo - ry be to God on high, and to the earth be peace;

good - will hence-forth from heaven to men be - gin and ne - ver cease.'
(earth)

Winchester Old from Thomas Este's *Psalter* 1592
Descant by Alan Gray (1855–1935)
Text: 'While shepherds watched their flocks by night' by Nahum Tate (1652–1715)

100a WOODLANDS

'Lift up your hearts!' We lift them, Lord, to thee

Descant by Richard Lloyd

Then, as the trum - pet-call, in af - ter years,

'lift up your hearts!' rings peal - ing in our ears,

still shall those hearts res - pond, with full ac - cord, 'we lift them

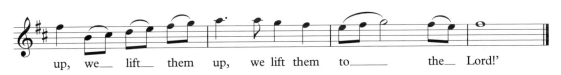

up, we lift them up, we lift them to the Lord!'

100b WOODLANDS

Tell out, my soul, the greatness of the Lord

Descant by Benjamin Lamb

Tell out, my soul, tell out the glo - ries of his word! Firm, firm is his

pro - mise, and his mer - cy sure. Tell out, my soul, tell out his great -

-ness to child ren's, child - ren's child - ren for ev - er - more!